THE
JEWISH REFLECTION
JOURNAL

CHRONICLE BOOKS
SAN FRANCISCO

ISBN 978-1-4521-5765-8

Manufactured in China

Text by Drew Cohen and Kelly Cohen
Design by Alice Chau

10 9 8 7 6 5 4 3 2 1

Chronicle Books LLC
680 Second Street
San Francisco, California 94107
www.chroniclebooks.com

L'CHAIM

Introduction

The holidays on the Jewish calendar provide a framework for the year, each with its own celebrations and practices. With so many ritual items and actions, so much to "do," it's easy to view Judaism as an external practice that is only about going through those motions. But for all the physical action, there are parallel opportunities for mindfulness. Using the tools and ideas of Judaism, we can develop a richer internal life and a connection to ourselves.

Jewish ritual operates in cycles of time—from daily practices to the year-long calendar—and these cycles have the potential to give structure to our lives. In addition to all the external aspects of each celebration, Jewish holidays present us with unique opportunities for personal reflection as well. The themes and ideas of the holidays take us through a series of yearly spiritual opportunities. We celebrate new beginnings on Rosh Hashanah and finding light in the darkness during Chanukah. Each holiday is attuned to its specific season, with unique themes and principles. The yearly cycle of celebrations keeps us in touch with the natural world and provides markers throughout the year for self-examination and celebration.

This journal helps to bridge the gap between Judaism's ideas and the mindful reflection that leads to personal growth. Each Jewish holiday is explained and accompanied by a writing prompt and celebration tip, so you can dig into the aspects of those days that have the greatest potential for thought and meaning. Quotes from Jewish text and tradition are jumping-off points for thinking about your own life and experience.

Before all the Jewish daily prayers were fully composed, individuals improvised their own prayers on specific themes, including health, unity, joy, forgiveness, and empathy. But hundreds of years later, many prayers in the prayer book are long, and their language foreign, inaccessible, or religiously off-putting. The barrier of Hebrew can be significant, yet as far back as the Talmud, Jewish legal authorities understood that for words to really connect with a person, they had to be in the language of that person's day-to-day life. And while prayer can be a form of guided meditation, so too can the practice of journaling serve that meditative purpose. Let this journal be an opportunity to check in with yourself, and get onto paper whatever it is you are holding on to in your mind.

Rosh Hashanah

Rosh Hashanah isn't just the start of the new Jewish year. It's seen as the World's Birthday. It is also the beginning of the High Holidays, and we are encouraged to begin a check-in with ourselves to see where we might have room for improvement or growth in the coming year. The holiday is celebrated with the sounding of the *shofar*, a trumpet fashioned from a hollowed animal horn. Honey is eaten to symbolize sweetness, in the hope that the year to come will be sweet and joyful.

The shofar we blow on Rosh Hashanah is meant to serve as a spiritual alarm clock—to wake us from ways in our lives in which we might be "asleep." How can you be more fully "awake" and in tune with the world and those around you in the new year?

It is not your duty to complete the work,
but neither are you free to abstain from it.

PIRKEI AVOT 2:20

Help me forge a oneness between myself
and others . . . help me forge a oneness of
the many selves within me.

RABBI NACHMAN OF BRESLOV

Let your house be open wide.

PIRKEI AVOT 1:5

Yom Kippur

A CHANCE TO START AGAIN

Yom Kippur marks the end of the "Ten Days of Repentance" that follow Rosh Hashanah. During that time we are asked to reflect on our past actions, committing to improve ourselves in the coming year and make the world a better place for everyone in it. The experience of the holiday is compared to a *mikvah*, or ritual bath—a kind of spiritual rebirth. We emerge from the holiday cleansed of the things we wish had been different in the past year, ready to make a fresh start in the coming year.

What would you do with a completely fresh start?

Free me of resentment against those who have wronged me. Help me abandon all the animosity, all the hostility that clogs my heart.

RABBI NACHMAN OF BRESLOV

No sin is so heavy that it may not be
repented of.

MOSES IBN EZRA

Forgive your neighbors [their] transgressions, so when you pray, your sins will be forgiven.

BEN SIRA 28:2

Sukkot

THE SEASON OF OUR JOY

Sukkot brings to a close the High Holiday season. After all the time spent in difficult internal reflection on Rosh Hashanah and Yom Kippur, Sukkot, known as the "Season of Our Joy," is an opportunity to be joyful that we've worked on improving ourselves, and a chance to take stock of our physical setting. Rosh Hashanah and Yom Kippur both focus on the impermanence of life, but Sukkot focuses on the impermanence of "stuff," with the building of a temporary hut, or *sukkah*, in which some people eat and sleep for the duration of the holiday. The sukkah is covered in natural materials (often bamboo or palm fronds) that don't entirely protect those within from the elements. The temporary sukkah lets us reflect on what is really important: not the "stuff" with which we fill our more permanent homes, but the joy of celebrating with those we love, surrounded by the simplest of structures.

What in your life brings you the most true joy? How might you bring more joy into your life?

CELEBRATION TIP: *Even if you aren't quite ready to move out onto the lawn or balcony for a week, Sukkot is a great opportunity to think about which things in your home are really essential, and to perhaps get rid of some of those things that do more to clutter than really enrich your life.*

Shout for joy, all that are upright in heart.

PSALM 32:11

If you are happy, the whole world benefits.

NETIV TZADDIK 71

To the counsellors of peace is joy.

PROVERBS 12:20

Simchat Torah

Simchat Torah is the end of Sukkot, and it
also marks the end of the annual cycle of
weekly Torah readings. The last few lines of
the book of Deuteronomy are read, immedi-
ately followed by the first lines of the story of
Creation from the beginning of the book of
Genesis, making a complete loop of the narrative. In many places, entire communities
dance with the Torah, celebrating together
our collective central narrative.

The stories of the Torah strike us differently at different stages of our lives as our experiences color how we see the stories. What is a story, song, or movie that has meant different things to you at different times? Write it down as a reminder to yourself of the power a shift in perspective can have.

Hatred stirs up strifes, but love covers all transgressions.

PROVERBS 10:12

Love your neighbor as yourself.

LEVITICUS 19:18

Help me turn my anger into love, and
enmity into compassion.

RABBI NACHMAN OF BRESLOV

Chanukah

THE FESTIVAL OF LIGHTS

Chanukah is celebrated primarily with candle-lighting during the shortest days of the year. The Rabbis transformed the historical story of a war between a group of Jews fighting both Greek assimilation and those Jews who chose to assimilate into the story of an extraordinary cruse of oil. It was an effort to highlight the miraculous and downplay violence, reframing the story into something more positive. What was seemingly only enough oil for one day shone for eight after the retaking of the Temple in Jerusalem by the Jews. The holiday's candle-lighting and delicious fried foods are all in commemoration of the miraculous oil.

Chanukah is Judaism's version of the universal impulse to bring light into darkness, to find meaning even in the most hopeless situation. In what ways might you bring more "light" into your life?

CELEBRATION TIP: *The lighting of the* chanukiah *(nine-branched candelabrum) is intended to publicize the miracle of Chanukah to the greatest number of people possible. You can light yours in your window for passersby to see, or throw a Chanukah party and gather friends and family to bring light into the dark of winter.*

We need an extra measure of compassion to understand and to care for one another with genuine sensitivity and with open acceptance.

RABBI NACHMAN OF BRESLOV

Honor every person, whether poor or rich, and let your thought be that you are honoring them because they are created in the image of God.

DERECH HAYIM 7:7

Why did the Creator form all life from a single ancestor? That the families of mankind should not lord ancestry over one another.

TOSEFTA SANHEDRIN 8:4

Tu Bishvat

A BIRTHDAY FOR TREES

Tu Bishvat, the new year of the trees, was once simply used to calculate taxes, but it has now become a holiday that celebrates nature in many creative and meaningful ways. Some view this holiday as a Jewish "Earth Day" and focus on ways to be more Earth-conscious, including planting new trees. Others choose to have a Tu Bishvat *seder*, a ritual meal where we eat different types of fruits that represent the different facets of ourselves: fruits with shells and peels, fruits with pits, fruits that are consumed entirely, and fruits (or spices) that are only smelled.

In the Tu Bishvat seder, fruits with pits represent internal hard places with potential for future growth. Find at least one "pit" that you struggle with which can be used as a catalyst for growth. How can you turn that difficulty into an opportunity?

Wisdom gives life to those that have it.

ECCLESIASTES 7:12

The more learning, the more wisdom; the more counsel, the more understanding; the more charity, the more peace.

PIRKEI AVOT 2:5

Who is wise? Those who learn from
all people.
PIRKEI AVOT 4:1

Purim

A CELEBRATION OF AUTHENTICITY

Purim celebrates the story of Esther, who, through seducing the Persian king, was able to avert a disaster for the Jewish people. She hid her Judaism to win the king's affection, but then revealed her true self in order to save the Jews from destruction. Purim is celebrated with a festive meal, a reading of the Purim story, gifting food to friends, and making charitable donations. It's a tospy-turvy holiday of frivolity and fun, celebrated with costume parties, sweet treats, and plenty of wine. There is a custom to drink oneself into a stupor, literally, until you cannot tell the difference between the story's hero and its villain. Of all the Jewish holidays, this is the time to party.

As part of their costumes, people often wear masks on Purim to hide their identities. This is a time to consider the "masks" we wear every day. How might you shed your own "mask" to be a more authentic version of yourself?

CELEBRATION TIP: *Part of the joy of Purim is recognizing how lucky we are to have so much and sharing that luck with those less fortunate. Now is a perfect opportunity to donate time or resources to charitable organizations in your community.*

All the world is a very narrow bridge, and the most important thing is not to be overwhelmed by fear.

RABBI NACHMAN OF BRESLOV

Not learning but doing is the chief thing.

PIRKEI AVOT 1:17

A person should never let their own small-
ness insignificance and humility cover
up their true greatness. For sometimes
a person downgrades himself to excess
and forgets that he still has many amazing
attributes.

RABBI NACHMAN OF BRESLOV

Passover

THE HOLIDAY OF OUR FREEDOM

Passover is the celebration of the exodus from Egypt, of moving from slavery to freedom. In the Passover seder, which traditionally begins the week-long festival, the story is retold in the first person, as if each individual at the table was there when it happened. The retelling of the journey from slavery to freedom is not meant to be just a story—it should inspire us to find new forms of freedom in our own lives. The food served at the seder is also part of the story. We eat horseradish and salt water to remind us of the bitterness and tears of slavery, *charoset*, a fruit mixture, to symbolize the mortar used by the enslaved Jews, and *matzah*, unleavened bread, to remember the rush in which the Jews left Egypt; they didn't even have time for the bread to rise.

The modern Passover seder reflects on slavery in many forms, both physical and emotional. Sometimes we are even slaves to ourselves and our own expectations. How can you free yourself from your internal demands?

CELEBRATION TIP: *Because of the emphasis on ridding one's home of* hametz, *or leavened products, the days leading up to Passover often include rigorous "spring cleaning." Even if you don't want to burn every last bit of bread in your house (although bonfires can be really fun), this is a great time to give your home a good once-over.*

Seek peace and pursue it.

PSALM 34

A merry heart is good medicine.

PROVERBS 17:22

Who is rich? Those who rejoice in their own lot.

PIRKEI AVOT 4:1

Shavuot

On Shavuot, we reenact the moment of
receiving the Torah at Mount Sinai, which
ultimately shaped the Jewish people. There is
a custom to stay up all night in preparation for
this awesome event so that we aren't caught
sleeping, physically or spiritually, when we
should be ready to receive meaningful insights.
(Interestingly, this custom seems to have
spread around the world about the same time
as the introduction of coffee.) Because the
plants and flowers of Mount Sinai were in
full bloom at the moment of revelation, there
is also a custom to bring plants into homes
and synagogues for the holiday.

One of the messages of the Torah is to recognize our universal inter-connectedness, that what one person does can have an impact on many others. Take a moment to reflect on the ways you're connected to the people around you. What can you do to bring more positivity to that connection?

CELEBRATION TIP: *Just like we brighten synagogues with plants and flowers, bring a new plant or two into your living space.*

Let the good in me connect with the good in others, until all the world is transformed through the compelling power of love.

RABBI NACHMAN OF BRESLOV

See, how good and pleasant it is for people
to dwell together in unity!

PSALM 133

Whenever you mention someone, anyone,
in conversation, make it a habit to bless
them with a good eye and a good heart.

DERECH HAYIM 7:8

Shabbat

Shabbat is a weekly opportunity to take a break—to let everything be for a while, and to act as if everything is exactly as it should be for 25 hours. It's a chance to check in with ourselves and our loved ones, unhurried by the pressures of the rest of the week. The beginning of Shabbat is marked by lighting candles, sharing a glass of wine, and breaking bread together. The end of Shabbat is marked with a ritual called *havdalah*, which means "separation." The wine and light from the beginning of the holiday reappear, along with the smelling of sweet spices, to take the sweetness of Shabbat into the week.

Shabbat is a time to separate from the chaos of daily life and reconnect with yourself and the people around you. How can you make space in your life to rest, rejuvenate, and connect with the things that are important?

CELEBRATION TIP: *One of the nicest things about Shabbat is the feeling of community created by sharing meals with friends and loved ones. Invite some friends or family members for a relaxed, delicious meal.*

Receive all people joyfully.

PIRKEI AVOT 1:15

Do justice, love mercy, walk humbly.

MICAH 6:8